# Longing Affections

**OrangeBooks Publication**

1st Floor, Rajhans Arcade, Mall Road, Kohka, Bhilai, Chhattisgarh 490020
Website: **www.orangebooks.in**

---



**First Edition, 2026**

**ISBN:** 978-93-7426-100-2

**Price:** Rs. 188.00



Printed in India

# LONGING Affections

TOM VARGHESE

OrangeBooks Publication
www.orangebooks.in

# Contents

1. Contents .......... v
2. Fragrance of Your Smile .......... 1
3. Love That Quantifies .......... 4
4. We Have No Time! .......... 6
5. Day Dreams .......... 8
6. Rush Hour .......... 10
7. Silent as Clouds .......... 14
8. Nobody's Listening .......... 16
9. That Forgotten Friend .......... 18
10. My Lady in Blue .......... 20
11. The Cursed Tree .......... 22
12. The World Inside .......... 25
13. I'm on My Way .......... 27
14. Being With You .......... 31
15. A Hug Away .......... 33
16. Seasons in My Heart .......... 35
17. Your Name .......... 37
18. Bleed .......... 39
19. This Night .......... 41
20. A Walk With You .......... 42

21. Stubborn Heart....44
22. Waves....46
23. Once More....48
24. Rain on Me....49
25. Toy Story....50
26. In a Cage....54
27. Sun of Nights....57
28. Not So Long....59
29. Round the Globe....61
30. Grand....63
31. Did You Know?....65
32. How it Feels…....68
33. The Reason I am Alive....71
34. Unheard....73
35. The Scary Nights....75
36. My Treasure....76
37. That Smile....78
38. Earn Your Goal....80
39. 'MINE'ing the Precious....82
40. Disappeared....84
41. The Devil in Me....86
**About the Book**....89
**About the Author**....90

# Fragrance of Your Smile

You, my bud
Which blooms with your smile
Spread the fragrance
As a garden of the world.

You, my bud
Which blooms with your smile
Spread the happiness
In an elegant style.

You, my bud
Blooms my eyes
Fills my heart
Which never dries out.

You, my bud
I wish you bloom
Throughout my life
Joy to my world
With your smiling smile.

You, my bud
Which my garden misses
To watch you smile
It is the beauty of my life.

You, my bud
I wish for all seasons
To travel to the valley
Where I can shed my fusses.

You, my bud
With all your petals
I keep counting
A thousand times.

You, my bud
Synthesise my joy
Peace and harmony
The moments I cherish.

You, my bud
Sprout your petals
Adding wings to my heart
Nectar me till you wither away.

You, my bud
Spread your smile
Bloom my life
Till I lose my soul.

# Love That Quantifies

You would drown in an ocean
Searching for love
Swimming together, you'll be a fool
Catch a whale, you got one love.

Walk together, you'll be lame
Take a ride, you'll be amazed
Hug all night, you'd get a stopover love
The sun is up; it was just a dream.

Kiss a day, the expiry is at night
A smile on, multiplies the affection
A week in darkness missed a smile
Fake the affection, you're valued.

Share the reality, you became absurd
Hilltop vacations gain three days of love
Unleash the sorrows, you've shown you're weak
Your strength is all when you're not yourself.

Make their dreams come true a day
All you got back was just a mirage
Until the next dream is made true
You'll be shuffled in the list of genres.

Follow your dreams, you'll be frowned at
Rainfall of distress and utter shame
Till your pockets get really deep
All you did was already erased.

Taking sacrifices, you were born in the 80s
Just do the shit, you are valid for a week
No patience, till all are accomplished
All your pains and efforts were in vain
The points you earned were misplaced in a void.

When your soul is away from earth
You'll never be missed nor remembered
Sell out the trust, in the void of actions
The playlists change, the endless pain remains.

# We Have No Time!

A goddess you are
Through the rusts and walls
The aroma fills and spreads through my room
Like a touch with your finger
Round and round.

A sight of you
Erase my darkness
A hug from you
Worth a thousand sleep
A kiss of yours
Gifts me a life, new to the world.

I miss a piece as big as the Earth
A hole in my heart
Pain of a heart attack
With your touches and kisses
I think all day.

To patch my heart
For you to flow
Feel my soul with the bare rosy lips
The warmth you give
Is a fire in the winter
Melts me down from all my temper.

Till we part, we hold our hands
Beyond, you have my heart
To the feet of your love, I pledge myself
I bow below the limitless affection
We have no time
Until we reunite next.

Your unconditional, blissful presence
Puffed my heart
With an all - time gift as favourites
The hugs and kisses and touches
Imprinted, that never fades away
Till we meet, I'll sleep in your heart.

# Day Dreams

Takes me through the unreal world
Past or future in front of my eyes
A dramatic world where I live in peace
Harmony is never at stake
All my wishes are accomplished.

There is no wrong
The whole world is right
A tilted universe we live to cherish
Time travels to make left, a right
The moments we chase
The extraordinary life
An escape from all reality.

Where dreams bloom into flowers
An endless snow and
Power to fly
Be the kings and queens
We make the rules.

We are the only Valentins
Breathe only love
Deserts and forests
Beaches and parks
It's just us, the world on our own.

Dances our way with the songs we love
A life beyond the horizon
Far, far beyond the stars in the skies
Without the spaceship, we would visit our universe.

The real world is hard to survive
Wish to elope where taste is all mine
Fly to the countries
For the endless memories
To make a lifetime full of joy
To distract ourselves from the pain of tears
Unload the burden of the real world.

# Rush Hour

We see no time
Days and weeks are at the speed of light
With a blink of an eye, months pass by
The age of sixteen was like yesterday
We see no moon, nor enjoy the sun
We form no image from the stars

Forgot to smile—we are never happy,
barely do what we love to do
Erased from the heart are the waves we counted,
climbed a rock, sang a song,
played the ball, escaped to the jungles—
moments with our soulmates—
All are distant memories.

We hear no birds chirping by the window
We go blind to the colours of nature
No blossoms bloom through the lanes we pass
We feed no fish or rabbits,
pamper no cats and dogs at home
The sound of rain is never refreshing
Now all burdened—yet we love it, but we forget.

We find no time to rejoice and rest,
but to catch time, we fly and run,
leaving behind all our loved ones,
to make their world and leave our dreams
Lifestyle is no longer a shopper's stop
And home is never a ground to pause
Stopped chasing what our loved ones loved,
lost all that we adore on earth
Hardly remember the names we love,
hardly remember the days to cherish—
It all ends up with a sleepless night.

Leaving the marks of dissatisfaction,
none of the checklists has been met
To impress strangers, we lost our loved ones,
controlled by unreal godfathers
We shake hands a hundred times,
but hold not the hands meant for us
Intimacy was months ago; initiative fades day by day
Kept aside is what we call humanity
What matters is to win unreal races,
for which we get erased in a day without traces.

We live as immortals, wasting all the time,
diminishing the world,
to a temporary relief,
living out silent, with a bag of grief
Sold our souls and surrendered as slaves,
to dumb affections,
explode passions—not to create one.

We save no time
We wait in the queue, with a trauma of hope
No other world but to rush ourselves
Hear no wars,
watch no nature,
smell no flowers,
sense no emotions,
and feel no love—
but fake our smiles to share their world,
to hold a colour from their flying colours,
where we live a lifc for the unknown ones.

The dreams we had are now influenced,
replaced and rewritten,
injected with leased passions
We strive through the changes—all in pain—
from the needs of unreal fathers
No space for empathy
Never do we think of lending a hand.

Our time, others' world, and their imprinted goals—
The holy book that buries us
Locked in a cage of selfishness
Yet we wish to be in paradise—
to laugh out loud and sleep at peace,
where time pauses for all joy,
to escape an analogue life,
set by a stranger, unsure of wisdom.

We beg the Almighty to take us away,
to free our souls and be in harmony,
and wish to have a dual time for all—
a fight for freedom from the faking smiles.

# Silent as Clouds

Watching all the unseen
Listening to the unheard
No one cares if they see or hear
Witness to all the war and peace
Sorrow and harmony of every living.

Travels throughout the world and time
Various dynasties watched all species endanger
Visiting countries, changing seasons
Through the fields and the snow - capped mountains
Heavy traffic and evergreen forests.

Over the oceans, Greenland, and Antarctica
When everyone looks up to pray
At times it wonders if it was the god
Shapeless, everywhere, anytime
Day or night, throughout the earth's life.

Watching all the unseen
Listening to the unheard
The only moving non living through all the nations
Is it you, the almighty?
Or is it you, the messenger to the immortal?

Never comes down, but watch from above
Archived from the prehistoric world
The secret to the tombs of Egypt
Wish I were as silent as a cloud
Your silence helped in mastering the truth.

You watched us from above, a true mastermind
The one who oversees the fate of all
Watching all the unseen
Listening to the unheard.

A silent shapeless beauty
Flowing foam of all the truth and lies
Are you the angel in the skies?

# Nobody's Listening

I had moved the mountains
But the city was asleep
I cried out loud, all were afar
When I laughed out loud
I was lost in space.

At times when there is someone around
I am forced to fake, but I bake to hate
I had lost my mind, lost my temper
Found no one to ask me why.

All I heard was an unfair life
To make them live with all the lies
Unfaithful to myself - the modern glory of life
To hide all truth and strive to deceive
Misleading emotions to fabricate life.

I found no one to ask me why
Unheard they stand, pointing me
Speechless they are, cursing me
Treats me as invisible, killing me
Ditched my emotion, brought a million smiles around.

Locked in the realm of the modern glory of life
To all those who seem to stand by me
It's yet another time for a bedtime story
Except for me, none really cared
I wish I had someone to tell why.

# That Forgotten Friend

Now, when I look back in time
It's merely a shadow of togetherness
We all have grown, we all have gone
Time or fate made us apart
We remember the name, but no emotion.

We had met somewhere, deep in past
Or either of us had a time travel
Barely remember, but we smile at each other
Diving deep to recollect the fun we had
All lost in the ocean of time.

Yet we remember the names we call
We sit together, no memories to share
An empty room with all unknowns
But we never forget to smile at each other
No words to utter, no story to start.

A mirage of fun we had in the past
Erased by time, the distance we had
A friendly stranger who knows the names
Both in different dimensions
With a ray of memories, we dance in the same hall
Was it me or was it them?

Who has changed? Who has gone? Who has grown?
A bare recollection of our names
The rest are erased by fate, time and distance
With no curiosity to meet again
We said goodbye for months or years ahead...

# My Lady in Blue

The one who finds a black in blue
Who stands by like the moon at night
Revolves as Venus, blue as Uranus
The blue water lake in the thickest forest
Clear as morning lightest sky blue.

Even though the clouds get through
She blooms the wisdom,
Fading the shady grey clouds
Bring us back the abundant sky blue
Beyond the reachable sea and sea beds,
She always remains far to hold.

The rarest colour, never being a typical blue
She will always be the blue diamond
The hardest to find and strong within
Yet she exists as vast as the oceans
An aquamarine in the ocean beds.

Often she is the turquoise stone
Heals, holds and binds with empathy
Here she is the softest blue gem
Yet so precious and priceless
She moves along the Mohs scale.

From turquoise to topaz to sapphire to diamond
To know her purity, an aquamarine
Smile as the blue diamond sparkles
She makes the world a clear, dark blue sky
Glitter our lives with shining stars.

Dazzling like a shooting star
We close our eyes to wish we owned her
As she would be the precious gem
We fly, trek, and dig the Andes
She's rare to find, like a bluc diamond and a blue opal.

# The Cursed Tree

On the night's lightning strikes
You stand so tall and strong and big
In the flash of lights
Glimpsed me a dark knight superhero
Admire to be who you are
Who holds our earth strong on the ground?

For decades and jubilees and centuries
Cover us from the radiant sun
Shield us from the enemy's heat
With the widespread hands
You wave a Hi, a billion times
With your tiny thousand fingers.

Why so silent? Why no move?
Why not play around with us all?
With your hundred lengthy hands
Nest the birds till they hatch and fly
Feeds the living throughout the season
In your presence, you help all breathe.

You teach your child to sprout and grow
Inculcate them to save and serve
Yet your family watch you fall
Emotionless and helpless, standing tall and strong
Without a goodbye, you break and slam on the ground
Why so hesitant? Why no reaction?

And shy to protest to all the mighty chainsaws
Till you fall, you feed them all
Bold you are through the decades
Watch the world, the change they make
The barren land and the smoggy morning
Yet not disheartened as death is close by.

A trillion good things you give us all
The only godly living idol on earth
Yet you are axed and uprooted
Make some noise or scare them away
Do you really wish, or do you sacrifice?
Ever shed a tear? Ever felt a pain?

You're the only living, offering free lunch
Till you dry, you serve us all
Though you do all unconditional favours
Your sapling watches your ravage
Homes to the birds and worms and bees
Are these the pieces of a furniture?

Cursed you are, not to cry and not to shout
And not to call out for help to save
Still, you stand so tall and strong
As a soldier guards the nation
The only guardian angel of the earth.

# The World Inside

To share more words if the sun never sets
Stare at your eyes to pause time
A day is beyond or a year shrinks to a day
Emotions playing games with my head.

I deeply fall like a Niagara fall
To an ocean bed of your own thoughts
Your glittering eyes outshine a star
Creates a space in my heart.

Welcome to the universe of my soul
The one and only star that shines
The only garden that blooms with all flowers
You fall like snow, in my dreamy nights
Like a sahara, hidden treasure and wonders.

You flood my heart, carry me away
I hold you tight like the forest roots
I swim in a pool of your warmth and affection
I hear you like the waves on the beach
Countless, endless, I listen to it all.

I wish time and life were infinite
Like your love, which heals my soul
We fly on cloud nine, round the globe
The bird's eye view of the world made me.

# I'm on My Way

Restless, I am without you
Here I booked a seat to come see you
The deepest unrest in my heart
Urges me to come see you
While I pack my bag for the bus
Till I get there, it will be a fuss
All I think is you and you and you.

You my drug has made me restless
Now my life is all pointless
I can't bear the deep unrest
It has been an immense pain
Which has made me more sightless
Now I am on board to come see you
All I see around is you and you and you.

As I look through the window
I can feel the wind on my cheeks
Like you caress on my cheeks
I wish you were here with me
I would hold you in my arms
And make you rest on my shoulders.

Everything I saw through the window
Gave me hope to see you soon
Bridges told me I am crossing borders
Signboards told me I am getting closer
Vehicles told me I will get there faster
Street lights gave me all the rays of hopes
The driver gave me full of hope
Yes, my love, I'm on my way.

When the bus got stuck in traffic
My pounding heart felt full of sickness
I prayed to the Lord to set us free
But thcn wc were there all evening
I closed my eyes to rest for a while
It brought my heart full of smiles
All I see is you and you and you.

When we made the turns and stops
I prayed to the Lord to show my love
Filled with hope, I look around
To find those glittering eyes of yours
My heart throbs to get there soon
But feel like I have been here for ages
When they look ahead, it's just a route
Driver sees the road ahead
All I see is you and you and you.

When the bus honks the way to you
I can hear you say, I love you
Throbbing me to fly to you
My heart sings the songs for you
With the blood and beats
Form the rhythms for you
Running through my nerves is you
All I think is you and you and you.

Yes, my love am getting closer
I don't want to wait any longer
Let us go for an adventure
To hold and watch you more closely
All I want is you and nothing better.

Yes, my love
I'm on my way.

# Being With You

Is a dream come true
Here I lie on your lap
Oh my god, what a fab
Sipping my love through your smile
Gazing at you gives me a smile
Melting my heart all the way down.

Your heart always plays the role
Of a remote to lure my soul
Senses you from far away
Directs me to where you are
Loving you so hard core.

Hugging you is my hobby
Holding you is so cosy
Staring at you, you're pretty
Changing life to such beauty
Watching you over is so lovely.

I will stand on my knee
Easy for you to hug me
I can hold you tight to me
In my arms you can lie
From where I can easily say
You took me all up away
Freezing my heart in May.

Cloud nine is where you took me
From where I see only you
Perfect spot for a lovely date
Let me take you much higher
You may feel it a bit deeper
To my heart, a bed of love
Where can you stay as long
Being mine forever long.

# A Hug Away

When your tears roll down
I stare at my blood bleeding out
Through my eyes you will see
A broken heart spilling blood.

Taking my soul up away
Making me a dead remain
Give me a chance, and I could try
To wipe your eyes fully dry.

Else I'll be a burning fry
O my love, please don't cry
Drown, I get in your eyes
Filling my heart with all the tears.

Blowing my heart, you could hear
May all sorrows come to me
Let you not bear the pain
Your smiling lips wash away.

All my pain like a saint
Yes, my Angel
The Magic wand is your smile
Just a smile and I'm alive.

You my precious
My only wealth
Making you so damn priceless
Nothing is worth stealing my heart.

Now you smile, and when you cry
Hurt me all the way you want
I would greet you with all my heart
Yes, I still love you so hard.

Lie on me and cry out loud
Prick me, bite me, burn me up
Punch me, bruise me, kick me down
Lastly, when you tear my heart.

You will witness a pool of love
Heal me with your smile and come
Here, I am a hug away.

# Seasons in My Heart

Blooming flowers in my heart
Fragrance of love all around
Diffuse to my blood and soul
Fragrance takes me out of the world
In my heart, you bring in spring.

Brighter love than the sunlight shines
With your thoughts, I've had sleepless nights
Melting my heart with your warmth
Drying my heart with your sun of love
In my heart, you bring in summer.

You, my daylight, don't grow short
Without you, I'll die of thirst
Missing you, I'll be in pale
Shed my soul with utmost pain
In my heart, you bring in fall.

Making nights the coldest ones
Tempting me to hold you tight
Blowing a blizzard in my heart
Rumbling down an avalanche of love
Frozen, I am in your arms
In my heart, you bring in snowfall.

Pouring love into my heart
Flowing through my arteries
Flooding my soul with all the love
In my heart, you bring in rain.

# Your Name

From where I stand
I fall back down
To a depth, never reaching down
Pausing time for all day long
Echoes your name deep within.

Gives a feel of a floating cloud
Missing heartbeats all the way down
Calms my mind with utmost peace
Close my eyes, now I see
Moments enjoyed with all the fun.

Brings joy to flavour my heart
Adding essence to my soul
While I fall, I know it's right
It is all the magic of love
Your name can complete love.

Builds your presence beside me
The way I walk around
Falling in love all the time
Hearing your name called from afar
Frozen, I stand for a sec.

I could see your pretty smile
Since your fragrance is all around
Filled with your thoughts in my heart
From where I stand
I fall back down.

# Bleed

Once I bloomed around with joy
You, my sunshine
Tell me why you stop to shine
Reason my heart kept on fire
Is left full of ash and smoke.

Not anymore, you rise and shine
Drying myself to a lifeless state
Like a man in outer space
Breathing through the void around
Left me in the darkness where
Not even the moonlight you spared.

On my knees, I stood on the ground
While my soul was taken with you
With a heavy heart, my love bleeds
Hustling myself with tearing pain
Keeping up the rage in heart
Not so much strength I have
Till I decay, I lie on the ground.

# This Night

Here I rest, my head on a pillow
Till I sleep to reach your dreams
All that comes
Are you in my mind?

Hold you closer to feel the warmth
Lifting you to dance on the floor
Sharing stories while I lie on your lap
Fistfights we have when I irritate you
The smile that makes me calm on sudden
Naughty kisses cherished for a lifetime
Oh, my queen, you bring colours to the dark
Making my dreams filled with love.

The only world, for now
Where we are one
Wish this sleep would never end.

# A Walk With You

Be it morning or at night
I stay blind to the world around
No matter how far we walk
I kept on seeing an endless road
May this moment stay forever.

No bright sun makes me sweat
No rain makes me drenched
Legs and feet never hurt at all
As long as I hold your hand and walk
Hold on tight to heal my wounds
Letting go will rip me apart.

Watching you smile so gently
Taking all my stress away
Making me watch the next sunrise
Be it through the morning traffic
Or through the city park, we roam in love
Fills my heart with drops of dew.

Silence in our conversation
Doesn't matter, till our fingers are locked
Staring at your sparkling eyes
The shining star that lights my world
May these moments never end.

Let the road take us down to hell
Still a heaven when you're aside.

# Stubborn Heart

Moving on without you
Is simple as walking from Earth to the Moon
Thoughts on being without you
In the state of breathlessness, I'll be
My dreams are filled with your smiling face
Right till before I fall asleep
Every song I listen to
Takes me to the middle of the sea
Where do I see your presence around?

Diving into the ocean of your thoughts
I float around, close my eyes
The moments we had act as waves
Taking me to a prosperous shore
Where all my wealth is in your musings
Even when I open my eyes
I can see your presence nearby
Feels the hug you always gave me
While I try to get some sleep.

When I try to listen to things
All I hear is only your voice
Lost in the woods of your ponder
Where I love to get trapped often
As I roam around the places
Your musings are what I wish to carry.

Everything I see around
Reminds me of your loveliness
Everything I see around
Has been filled with your memories
Painful indeed to carry around
The same gives me the strength to walk till death.

# Waves

I always find myself at the beach shore
Bringing back all your moments
Waves after wave, you float to me
Splashing me with all the lovely age.

Through the horizon, I can see you rumble
Like your thoughts give me trouble
What I see when I open my eyes
All your memories are like the waves
Spread across the widest world
Showed me that you were my world
Proved that you were always my soul.

Mostly, you give me a gentle touch
Sometimes you hit to push me back
At times, you make me imbalanced
Certain big ones tip me off
On purpose, I move to the depth
From where your thoughts can float me away
From the reality in your absence
To a wonderland to feel your presence.

# Once More

I saw you once
Is like a million times
In my heart, as hard as a diamond
Dispersed into a million lights
Even as I close my eyes
I can see that diamond
Shine so bright.

Shining always brighter than the sun
Never setting down from my heart
Once more, I wish to see you soon
You will remain in my thoughts
Even though I lose my soul
The diamond will shine brighter than the sun
You, my diamond, be my soul!

To be the one
Hard to find.

# Rain on Me

As all those clouds get so heavier
Fills my heart with the coldest breeze
From afar I can hear you fall
Waiting for you to rain on me.

Staying drenched as you are all over me
It's all you I see around, each drop
That flows into me is a portion of love
Which I feel you are all over me.

I don't run, nor do I cover
I want you to run from my head to my toes
Once you finish bursting at my heart
I wait till you rain on me again.

To cleanse me, in and out
With your spell and magic wand of love.

# Toy Story

All my toys were always vehicles
They all played with balls and bats
I kept making highways on sand
Roads and bridges through the garden
Driving my car through the bush
Making my own hill stations
Always near a bus station.

Gifting a toddler a remote car
From there added one by one
If it were only Mercedes
Nothing below never ridden
Then I owned the whole of the road
I was then the king of roads
What I owned was a car to a plane
Then I owned from truck to train.

They all made my bed to sleep
I kept making bed-highways
They all slept by hugging a pillow
I slept, parking trucks below
When the others brushed their teeth
Rolling buses were my tea
Speeding my car through the bed-way
Trucking loads to the railway station
Which was always near a bus station
From my plane I look all down
Watching over my own town.

Bushes were my forests always
Bricks were always buildings to me
Heep of sand were the hill stations
On the ground, I made my town
Wherein I made my own rules
From the boxes I made trains
I was always entertained
Hitting cars was on purpose
I kept saying, it's my own town.

Even when I step out of my home
Thinking that I am going to Rome
I keep my ride in the palm
Driving through the walls and sand
Taking my dreams to Amsterdam.

Flying back on my own airlines
Sailing oceans in my own cruise line
Round the globe in such an ease
Not knowing what a passport is
Crossing borders with such a craze
Till I sleep, I keep my race
More than being a conglomerate
Always made my days complete.

Once I had a sea of toys
Cars and trucks were all around
Buses and trains were rolling around
Planes and ships were floating around
You all made my days very short
Gave me heart to love the engines
Now I have the real engines
But toys are all I imagine
Now I stand with nothing left
Missing days of the King of roads.

# In a Cage

Fly like a bird and spread your words
You were born in this world
To make your own
Path to dreams
Show'em all your wings to fly
Let'em watch you fly so high
Conquer your space in this world
Chase the dreams with all your might.

May all be small or big
Once you differ from others
Not all will lend you a hand
Instead, they will pull you down
Cursing you in prayers all the time
All they want is for you to be them.

They might start pelting stones
They will speak in various tones
Even some might break your bones
Frustrations can be seen at home.

Not even your siblings know
What you love is what you do
Only a part of what they say
Always remain right for you.

Even those who gave you birth
Often stay on the other side
Blaming you for not being them
Acting for them is what they want
Pushing yourself not to be you
Not realising what you are
What do you have
And what you did
What they say is what they saw
With their eyes and not with yours.

Yes, they all will scramble you
Tear your heart into bits
Playing games with emotions
Making the deepest scar in you
Wounds that stay forever in you
It might seem to lose your charm
Friends turn foes in no time at all
Painful till you prove them wrong.

Eating food for your own hunger
Drinking water for your own thirst
Sleeping for your own rest
Working out for your own health
All is done for your own need
Enrich you with joy and rejoice
Why not work for what you love?

Like the sun that shines each day
Reach a milestone at the end of the day
Setting hope high in the sky
Breaking the cage of someone's wish
All you need is the strength of mind
They all made their dreams come true
Gained all the happiness in their life
Wealthy till they stay alive
Why not start chasing dreams?
Why not do what you love?

# Sun of Nights

As the daylight sets in the night
Peeping at us through the clouds
Smiling with your crescent phase
You start shining close to Earth
Watching us through the woods.

Such a broad mind in you have
You know you don't own the shine
You share all you get from the sun
In your heart, you possess beauty
No wonder you shine so pretty.

Heart to give out all you have
Without making your own shine
Wish we all had a heart like yours
To lead us to a prosperous life
Lighting up the streets at night.

In case one lost their way
Even when none is around
Clouds pass and take light away
Still, you shine with hope set high
Yet to learn a lot from you
Often wondered if you were a lord
Watching us through the dark.

Each night, you show a different phase
Without losing your pretty face
Showing signs of being an introvert
Once a month, you hide yourself
Wonder what you do that night.

Glancing at you through my window
Hide and seek is what we play
Even though you hide on clouds
With all pride, you shine out bright
Spreading beauty to the night
Lighting darkness within us.

# Not So Long

Till we exist, we will conquer
Bringing you down one by one
Once the day lights from the east
Cutting branches, falling trees
The noise of the chainsaw wakes me up.

Through the coast, a river view courtyard
Narrows down your course of stream
Building houses is our dream
Now that we can walk across
You are trapped in a dam for a long.

My dear mammals, reptiles, and birds
Have the will to face your doom
Last one will be caged till death
That fine feathers and horns and bones
Will remain, for the time to come, nailed to the walls.

Mountains no more cap a snow
A few might miss a scenic "wow"
Paving way so flat and straight
All we want is to move with ease
Making sure we uproot all
Hope Mother Earth will be a sphere.

Selfish is what stands so tall
Earning is what was always told
Foster fame is what we were taught
Not so long, you'd let us know
Without you, we shall not live long.

Too late, we are
Humans need to learn
To sustain all is why made us for
We are hidden and covered
With a blanket of Selfishness.

# Round the Globe

Keep on going is my motto
A life full of journeys is my dream
Stepping down at all the stops
Exploring the facts, of all places
Round the globe I wish to go!

Let the bus, train or flight
Places and routes are the same
Once the journey starts on time
Every place shows its own beauty
Each journey has its own story.

End of lines is a different world
Gives an adventure for life
Step by step, as I proceed
Takes me far from being inhumane
Not so far I've been these years
Yet I feel I've gone all around
As I pedal through the town.

Rich I am, with the happiness
Day or night, it doesn't matter
Round the globe I wish to go!

Miss those days I set to go
Drive my fingers through the maps
Checks on scheduled trains and buses
Joyful knowing they run on time.

As they move on to the points
Makes me onboard in my thoughts
Close my eyes to see the cities
Passing through the river and valleys
Watching plains while climbing hills
Through the coast I watch the sea
Gusty winds that pamper the face.

Even though I sit at home
Honking cars and trucks, I hear
Wishing people a happy journey
All the roads and rail across
Reaching out to the nukes of nation
Round the globe I wish to go!

# Grand

The only proven love I've ever felt
Even though you never hold my hand
Secured, I was in your presence
The ones who showed me who to trust
Unconditional and assured concern
The reason I was blind while being with you.

With your affection, you proved it wrong
My first love was never my parents
Caring was what all about
The voice of pure love was always heard
Each time you called me from afar
All the mischief I did as a lad.

Was forgiven like a lord from heaven
I miss sitting on your lap
Like a prince with all the pride in heart
Now that we stay far, far away
It takes a lifetime to reach so high
Among the stars, you hide in clouds.

With all the magic of love in your hands
You will retain the lesson of love
In my books of life on earth
Till my end, your influence remains
Fathers with such grand powers
The very first miracle in my life.

The only one who showed me past
Connected me to the present and future.

# Did You Know?

O my precious...
Where are you?
It's been a long time, I heard from you...
Do you know how much I miss you?
You know how much I think of you?
Since I am staying away from you
I should remind I care for you.

I always wished you had never left me
All I think is your return
Heart felt heavy when I saw you going
Broke my heart to know your late return
Now I know how far my soul is
Time couldn’t teach me to be without you.

Even though we talk over the phone
It was never the same while you were here
If I get a chance to be with you
I would fill you up with hugs and kisses
Of course, I will get your favourite chocolates
Only if you are here with me.

Yes, I know we don't have much to talk
All things are the same here and there
I am happy that you are free from disease
All I want is you back, safe.

Ask me how I miss you now
I would say that I'm a fish that washed ashore
The one who is struggling to breathe
I miss the smile you give me
Which always greeted me like a welcome drink
I miss the louder laughter you have
Which makes me happy from the other corner.

I miss listening to the louder talks,
Which always makes the room alive
I miss flying kisses from your corner
Which always makes my day complete
I miss the graceless looks on your face
When I wear the outfit you dislike.

I miss the bye-bye you say with our fingers
Which makes me feel I'm in luck to have you
I miss the arguments we have all the time
Which always turns out to be the sweetest
I miss buying chocolates for you
Which I have always done with pride.

Even though you came late to my life
Even though we have never been together
Even though I shared things with others
Even though I have been with others
Even though you are placed far from me
I always wished to spend time with you, out.

At least walk you to the bus stop
But our work never let do so
Even though they are all there
Of them all, you are my gem
With the tiny memories you gave me
It helped to fill my heart with love.

O, my precious
All I want is you back, safe
At least I could watch you daily smile.

# How it Feels...

A blink of an eye
The sun already sets
A lifelong story
Envisions through my eyes
I forget my mother
I forget my father
I forget myself.

As I watch your eyes
That plays the role of seasons
It fills my flesh, all fantasies around
Flying like fireflies
Lights up my darkness.

The way you dance
The way you kiss
The way you hold my hand in public
In my dream world
Holds my breath in the real world.

There I faint
And fall into deep
Onto your heart
Deep as pacific
Sediments on your heart corner floor.

I forget the world
I forget the time
I forget the place
All and when your thoughts pile up
I fly as high
Into a hallucinated world.

Where you design
Shape, colour, and garden
Sun and moon
Beaches and hills
Where we stand to behold the stars.

Waves in the ocean
Wind in the desert
Droplets in the rain
Memories and dreams.

Twinkle like the stars from the sky
Drawn a constellation of our love
In my heart and life and soul
Enlightens the world we drew
Where you shine like a billion - year sun.

# The Reason I am Alive

When the clock ticks twelve
You start the day with a piece of chocolate
Licking fingers till my heart gets full
Fills my soul with your prettiest smile
The time I start to be there for you.

Even when the sky is about to rain
I was able to count the stars
From the counts and shapes you shared
You draw the Orion, Aquila, for my emotions.

My heart tunes itself to hear you near
All the way I drive back home
Your aura of presence never lets me alone
Where I wish I would never reach back home
And the road never ends, and time stays paused.

Oh my, gem, I want to see you sparkle
Which keeps the flame in me alive
Gives me a smile for no reason
Pinned my day with your memories.

As we walk down the streets
The silence makes me listen to your heart
As I look ahead, the streets
I see you playing around my heartbeat
The reason why I am still alive.

# Unheard

Unseen as a ghost
The pain is never realised
Unlit as the moon in a day
Hidden in the lights of co-existent morals
The inner turbulence
Quakes that kills our self.

Death happens cell by cell
Burning organs into ashes
Implodes the body, leaving no soul
We rage as an unforeseen hurricane
Unseen to them, emotions flying in the air
Crumbles down the world in front.

To them, we are a self - made disaster
A shaken, self - ignited, in the dark
Bounded by the unforgettable
Downpour of our losing senses
Thorns in the head, deep within.

Holding on to an overfilled heavy heart
Ranging emotions in utter silence
Paints our happiness
With pounding, bursting heart
The pain remains unheard.

# The Scary Nights

It's always night when I step out home
All the time I realise the same
Even though there are millions near me
What I see is an empty road
Leading me to a lonely round.

I can see a few pass by
Not noticing me as it's dark
Where I sit is an empty park
Where the birds forget to chirp
Till this time, it has been the same
All I have seen are passersby.

As if my life is an empty highway
Rushing to reach where they wish to be!
Till they get swallowed by the deck
I watch them from the scary park.

# My Treasure

There you are, beside me, where I sit
Leaning out all your sorrows
Fading away as I hold you tight.

There you are, curled up behind me
Confused me with your joy or sorrow
Eroded as I turned to ask.

There you are, all alone
Facing the endless sight
Erased away as I ran to you.

There you are, in my dreams
Giving me the sleepless nights
Fades away as I open my eyes.

Here I am, open to hearing from you
Be it while we get drenched in rain
Be it while we burn in the sun
Here I am, to hear from you.

There I am, to wrap you around
None of your joy gets away
Never let that smile corrode away.

# That Smile

With your smile,
Oh, my love!
Hopeful than a morning sunshine
You leave an ocean of happiness
To my soul and through my nerves.

As you start to smile out from sad
Boosts me to live a million lives
Your smile can fill the silence around
Pleasant, I am in your presence.

Watching you smile is my favourite hobby
Which makes me sit by your side
Billionaire I'm, while I watch you smile
With your smile, you enlighten my world
Makes me forget I am on earth.

The only moment I felt so blessed
Is only when I see you smiling around.

# Earn Your Goal

The journey of life starts with an aim
Showing you to conquer the world
The one that keeps you smiling till death
Bloom you with the happiness in life
Climbing the ladder of life
Where others can't chase you down.

The one that can draw your happiness
Is to achieve the goals you set
From a toy car to an empire
Journey is based on what you set
The man with no goal
Are the slaves of the desert.

Sand dunes take all the dreams away
Sprouting no seeds into a life
Dry and dead are all that's left
Not to perish a day or night
To spread like the Sahara, with all the ruined dreams
Losing all its fertility, helping you not to grow.

To bring back life is not worth
Life is all about making goals
Goals are to chase them down
Conquer them to make you happy
That is the essence of life
Fulfils one's own destiny.

# 'MINE'ing the Precious

I found you lost in the mud
My instinct told me you would glow
As I rain on all over you
I saw you sparkle beneath the dirt
No, No, No would harm you in any way
Nor take you away from my sight.

I have picked you up and washed away
All your dirt and hurt and wound
Make you my gem and guard you
Days and nights like a dark knight
You're my one in a million one
Would remain precious than all the queens.

You would remain my diamond star
Day and night with the doze of my love
From the rust, I'll make you shine
Here I'm to hold your hand
To make you move on and on.

You are now, and you'll always be
You, my one in a million one.

# Disappeared

Flew away as I opened my eyes
My heart sank, and as cold as ice
At times, I bleed, and I cannot sustain
A glacier of memories which never melts
I feel the lips when the breeze blows by
Out in the dark, I hear your whisper.

Close my eyes, I see you never cry
Shining my day and nights with a storm of thoughts
In all the noise, I hear you out
Pounding my heart to shout out loud
You flew away as I opened my eyes
Out to sorrow, despair and loss.

Tell me, can I be in your arms?
Starving with an obsession
Ends my day on admiration
Sweetest dreams of all my nights
My better half blooms my dusks
You flow as an ocean.

On the horizon, far, far away
Akin to rainbows, hardly be touched

# The Devil in Me

You were saved
Remember, from the swamp of mud
With all the dirt
You left me with rage.

I tried to mend
Broken heart and a lost life
Trapped in chaos and emotional blackouts
Now witness my vengeance throughout.

I'd lend my hand to uplift
Rebuild a life
From all distress and regrets
Poisoned me with freezing blood.

A disordered life to bloom with dreams
I crushed my dreams and hopes
Back to the drawing board to design our life
The rays of hope and dreams.

We saw that we grow beyond the skies
All my efforts, all in vain
Definitely, not for a lifetime
The pain I suffered.

Remain in my blood
But, for a lifetime
The unlearned lessons
New chapters and pages.

Reshaped my life
Melting down my frozen blood
Never in my far-far thoughts
You remain, erased from all.

For once, I lived for all your Wisdom
Unboxing the gift, I got
I was never a part of life
Yet, I feel, I have done.

A million times
Through all my thoughts
Thrashed you hard
Crushed in my fist.

Slit your throat
Rip and tear, you apart
Burned you alive
All the nights and days I live.

Now, I cut you loose
Face your fate
With the pinch of emotion
Till we unhitch, for the better.

# About the Book

*Longing Affections* is a heartfelt collection of poems that journeys through the many shades of human emotion—love, longing, distance, nostalgia, and self-reflection. Each poem captures fleeting moments and lingering feelings that often go unspoken, yet deeply felt.

At its core, this book explores the intensity of connection—how a single presence can bring meaning, how absence can echo louder than words, and how memories shape the way we experience the world. From the warmth of companionship to the ache of separation, the verses reflect both the beauty and fragility of relationships.

Beyond romance, the collection also touches on life's broader realities—lost time, changing priorities, silent struggles, and the quiet battles within. Poems question the pace of modern life and the cost of chasing expectations, while others offer an escape into dreams, nature, and imagination.

Written in a simple yet evocative style, these poems invite readers to pause, feel, and reconnect—with their own emotions, their memories, and the people who matter most. Whether it is love that uplifts or pain that lingers, *Longing Affections* becomes a space where every reader may find a reflection of their own story.

This is not just a collection of poems—it is a journey through the heart, where every word seeks to be felt rather than merely read.

# About the Author

Tom Varghese is a passionate writer whose words are deeply rooted in emotion, memory, and introspection. Through his poetry, he explores the subtle yet powerful experiences of love, longing, distance, and the quiet battles within the human heart.

His writing reflects a keen observation of life—capturing both the beauty of intimate connections and the complexities of modern existence. Whether expressing the warmth of affection or the weight of unspoken pain, his verses aim to resonate with readers on a personal level.

Drawing inspiration from everyday moments, relationships, and inner reflections, Tom's poetry creates a space where emotions are not just expressed, but felt. His style remains simple, honest, and evocative, allowing readers to find pieces of their own stories within his words.

*Longing Affections* marks his journey of turning emotions into expression—offering readers a glimpse into a world shaped by love, dreams, and the search for meaning.